The Hen in the Pen

Paige Cornetet

Illustrated by Max Rambaldi

Throughout her childhood, Paige's father held "dad's classes" to help his children understand a variety of financial concepts. The ideas from those classes inspired her to write a series of children's books to simplify complicated concepts such as debt, principal, talents, taxes, and the economy. She believes exposure to these concepts at an early age gives kids a head start in grasping more complicated financial concepts later. She hopes her books will clarify these themes for kids—and knows that if kids can grasp them, anyone can.

Contact Information
paige@spendthen.com
616-443-1000
www.spendthen.com

The Hen in the Pen

by Paige Cornetet

Copyright © 2019 by Paige Cornetet.
All rights reserved.
Printed in the United States of America.

Illustrations by Max Rambaldi.

No part of this book may be reproduced, stored in a retrieval system, or transmitted in any form or by any means, electronic, mechanical, photocopying, recording, scanning, or otherwise, except as permitted under sections 107 or 108 of the 1976 United States Copyright Act, without the prior written permission of the author.

This book is dedicated to my Farmor Karen Fessel.

Thank you for teaching me that it is better to work hard than to touch my principal. I'm grateful for you being the matriarch of our family.

Mrs. Spend-Then
Married a farmer
And let me tell you
He was quite a charmer.

As time continued on,
Their flock was bigger than one could project.

Talking Points

Why are the eggs important?

What are the chickens?

What happens when the cat eats the chicken?

What does Mr. Spend-Then teach Mrs. Spend-Then?

How many chickens are in the book?

What happens when the couple focus on the flock?

Who are Mrs. Spend-Then friends who help collect the eggs?

How many different color overalls does Mr. Spend-Then have?

Notes

SPEND-THEN

Contact Information

paige@spendthen.com

616-443-1000

www.spendthen.com